Maria Ivashkina

I Feel That Way, Too!

Komorebi, Sobremesa, Gezellig

to trust the wind, the excitement, the wave,
to remember forever these moments,
when you do forget which country you are in
and start to remember the planet

Vera Pavlova

I sit in my smultronställe, almost on the roof, at night—
only the sky above my head and a lonely bright star.
Where are you now? What color is your sky? Maybe you also look
at this star, which means that we are together and feel the same thing.
Like all people in the world. And there is not much difference between us
because everyone speaks the same language—feelings, gestures, touches,
intonations, views. Sometimes you see how a person is smiling
or looking, and you know that you share the same experience.

Different languages have very precise words for complex feelings.
Each country is like a person with its own character.
By putting such words together, you can draw a portrait,
describing the whole country with the mix of these unique feelings.

Surely, some of these words and feelings will sound familiar. But others
might surprise you and help you notice special moments in the future,
such as how sunlight shines through the leaves. And maybe these feelings
and words will become yours. In the end, it doesn't matter what you call it;
the main thing is that you mention it and feel.

strikhedonia
(strikhedohneeah)

the joy of being able to drop your work and not think about it further

craic
(crack)

a feeling of community. To feel craic, you need to be among the people with whom you feel most comfortable.

UNITED KINGDOM

hiraeth
(heerite)

a longing for a place you can't return to

coorie
(cooree)

to curl up, to nestle; a feeling of comfort and warmth

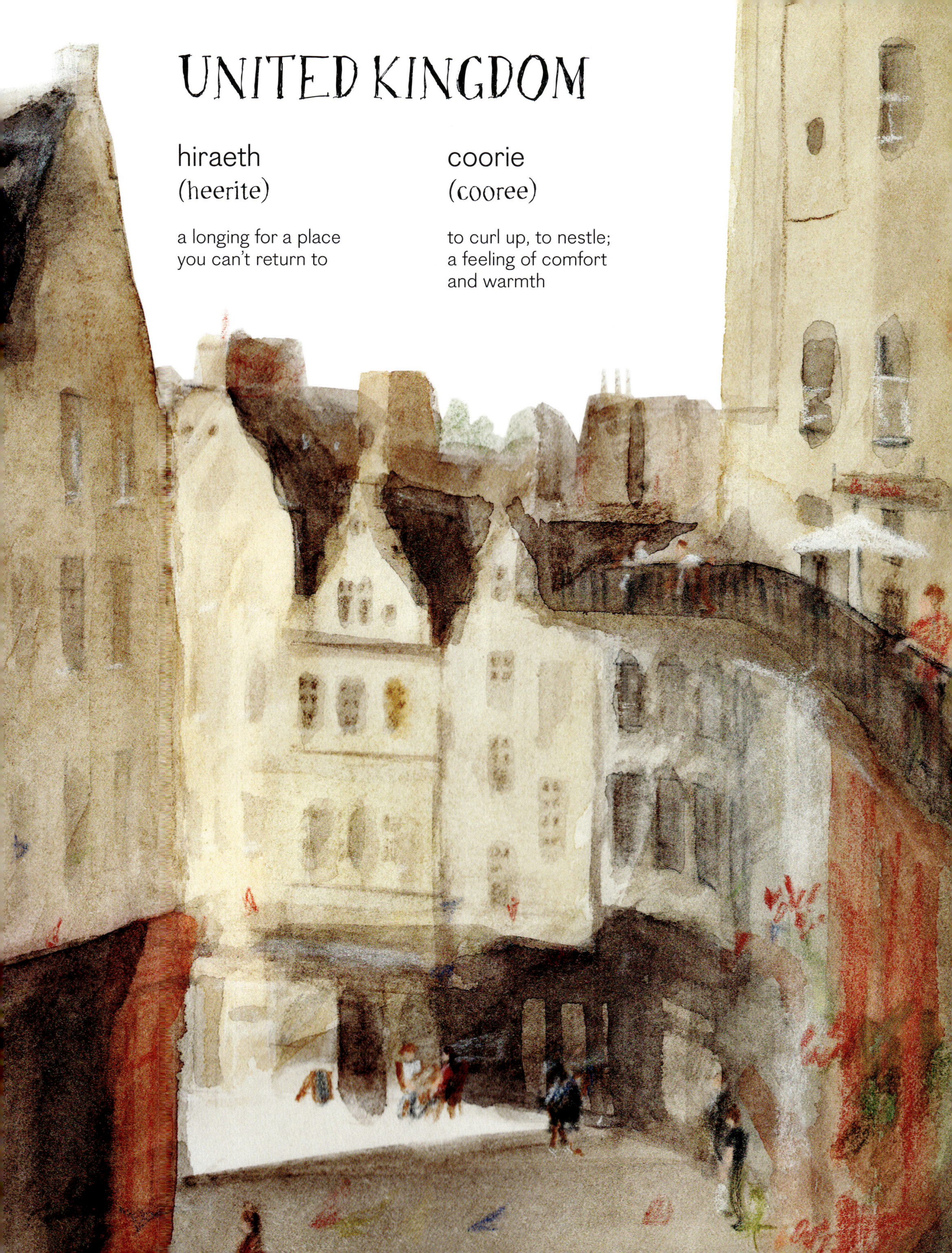

GERMANY

Fernweh
(fiernvay)

the call of faraway places; yearning for the places you have never been to

Torschlusspanik
(torshloosspanik)

a fear of missed opportunities and time slipping away

Blueschtfaehrtli
(blooshtfairtlee)

a flower ride; taking a slow car ride to enjoy the spring blossoms

Waldeinsamkeit
(valtaynsamkite)

unity with nature; when you are standing alone among the trees and feeling as if you are the only person on the planet

Sturmfrei
(shturmfrriy)

the freedom to do what you like because you are home alone and nobody is watching you

Geborgenheit
(gehborgenhite)

the feeling of complete safety, warmth, care, trust, and love

φιλοξενία
(philoxenia)

hospitality and respect for strangers; the joy of meeting a new person

βόλτα
(volltah)

to walk without a goal, wandering and enjoying the sights and sounds

περατζάθα
(peratzatha)

the peaceful state gained by watching people

chōros
(choros)

an intimate place where you can return to find yourself

GREECE

μεράκι
(meraki)

to give all your heart and soul to any act and to dissolve in the process. Meraki has no limits because you can be devoted to any casual activity, such as making coffee with love for someone.

morgenfrisk
(mornfrisk)

the feeling of cleanliness
and freshness from waking up
well-rested at dawn

DENMARK

hygge

(huegah)

to get pleasure from everyday activities; the ability to appreciate simple things like a delicious breakfast, meeting with friends, or watching a movie

arbejdsglæde

(arbidesglil)

happiness at work; to enjoy the job you are doing, regardless of how well-respected your profession is

طرب

(tahrab)

to be enchanted by the music. Tarab is a certain kind of pleasure you feel when listening to good music. It takes you to another place, makes you shiver, and lifts you up from the ground.

EGYPT

سمر

(sahmar)

to stay with friends and talk until late, long past the sunset

روقان

(rookan)

the mindfulness coming from doing something without hurry, in a way which allows you to enjoy it

विरह
(viraha)

love, the understanding
of which comes with separation

ناز
(nuz)

the pride and confidence that
come from understanding you
are loved unconditionally

INDIA

जुगाड़
(jugaad)

improvisation and resourcefulness.
By thinking outside the box,
you can do more with less.

ICELAND

Þetta reddast
(teehhta reddast)

everything will get better; everything will work out; the confidence that you can find a way out of any situation

sólarfrí
(sohlahfree)

a sunny weekend; the time when workers are given rest to enjoy the sun and warmth

að nenna
(arth nennah)

persistence to resolve any issue despite how complex or boring it is

gluggaveður
(glookavedhurr)

window weather; the kind of weather that would be pleasant to watch through the window, but not to experience outside

vivir al día
(veevir al dia)

to live for today because the most important things are happening now; not to hold back any emotions. If you want to laugh out loud—laugh; if you want to cry—cry.

SPAIN

sobremesa
(sobremaysah)

a moment when you have finished eating together, but everybody stays at the table to talk despite the empty plates

vacilando
(vakhilando)

a journey in which the process itself is more important than the final destination

ITALY

meriggiare
(merrijahrri)

to avoid the heat of the midday sun by relaxing in the shade

arcigola
(artcheegoolah)

a slow feast; to enjoy the food and the act of eating

commuovere
(comovere)

to be deeply touched by someone's story

dolce far niente
(dolche far niente)

the sweet idleness where every minute is enjoyable, as is every activity. Dolce far niente is always about enjoying the moment. You don't have to feel guilty about wasted time because, in fact, it is full. Happiness is in a morning cup of coffee, a walk along the beach, and meetings with family and friends.

舍得
(sheeder)

to be ready to leave something and let it go

缘分
(yuanfen)

an irresistible force that brings people together; spiritual closeness and kinship

无为
(wuwei)

to let things go their own way without interfering. The clouds do not decide when there will be rain, they just wait until they are filled with water.

CHINA
乐极生悲
(lejishengbei)
the feeling of emptiness
after experiencing great joy

NETHERLANDS

gezellig
(khezellikh)

the sense that is created by time spent with loved ones, belonging to something greater than yourself. Anything can be gezellig—a picnic in the park, a boat ride, or a date in a cafe.

gunnen
(khunun)

to feel joy because somebody gets the blessings they deserve

weemoed
(vaymoot)

to find the strength
to overcome sadness

voorpret
(vorpret)

pre-fun; the anticipation
of the joy before the event
happens

uitwaaien
(oatvyeen)

to clear your head; to have a walk
and get rid of unnecessary thoughts

friluftsliv
(freelooftsleev)

life in the fresh air; a decision to stay in nature. Friluftsliv allows you to feel harmony with the world and yourself.

fjellvant
(fyellvarnt)

the habit of walking in the mountains. Climbing offers a goal, while physical activity brings joy.

forelsket
(forelzkut)

the inexpressible joy you feel when you fall in love with someone

NORWAY

peiskos
(piyskors)

the feeling of coziness from sitting in front of a crackling fireplace enjoying the warmth

gjensynsglede
(gyenseenglil)

the joy of meeting someone you haven't seen in a long time

etterpåklokskap
(ehtuhpuklukskarp)

the knowledge you gain from making a mistake

cafuné
(cahfooneh)

to gently run your fingers through a loved one's hair

desbundar
(dezbundar)

to go beyond one's limits; to get rid of inner fears

desenrascanco
(dehzenhasscanso)

the ability to get out of difficulties even when you didn't have a good chance of succeeding

saudade
(sowdhade)

bright sadness for something much loved, but that is irretrievably lost or never existed. It can be a person, place, or thing. Saudade helps you to feel sharper; to live your emotions, rather than run away from them. Sadness is an important part of life. It is normal to be sad. It is happiness that has passed or did not happen.

PORTUGAL

myötähäpeä
(mooertuhhahpayu)

the feeling of shame felt for the ridiculous and stupid actions of others

sisu
(sisu)

demonstration of determination and resilience in difficult life situations; your internal ability to handle any challenge

FINLAND
raaskia
(raahskea)
to have
the courage
and strength
to do something

FRANCE

retrouvailles
(ruhtroovy)

to find each other again; the joy experienced from meeting after a long separation, not only in relation to a person, but also from returning to a favorite place

coup de foudre
(coo de foodrah)

a lightning strike; the breathtaking feeling when you suddenly fall in love with someone or something

dépayser
(dehpayzay)

the feeling of something new that you experience from an unusual situation in another country

esprit de l'escalier
(esspree de lesskaleeay)

the wit on the stairs; a feeling when only after a conversation you understand exactly how to answer someone

joie de vivre
(jwa de veevruh)

life is already a reason for joy. It is thankfulness for an opportunity to move, see, or feel the warmth of the sun or the touch of a friend.

SWEDEN

lagom
(laargom)

not a lot and not a little,
just as much as you need

fika
(feekah)

a time to get together, chat,
and have a coffee with a dessert

resfeber
(reesfeebur)

a restless state full of anxiety and expectation
just before the start of a journey

smultronställe
(smooltronsteleh)

a strawberry field. This word is used to describe a favorite place where you can hide from the world and be alone with yourself—everyone has their own special place.

gökotta
(jerkotah)

an early-morning cuckoo; to wake up early in the morning and hear the first birds singing

JAPAN

生き甲斐
(ikigai)

the meaning of life
that makes you wake up
in the morning

阿吽
(ahun)

an understanding without words
between the closest friends

木漏れ日
(komorebi)

happiness from seeing the sun's rays coming through the leaves

恋の予感
(koi no yokan)

a premonition of love; the feeling at the first meeting that falling in love is inevitable

Most of all, I want us to focus on our feelings, to live them, to look at them from all sides and enjoy them. Idleness is a word with a negative meaning in the Russian language, but at the same time it describes a moment when there is an opportunity to understand what is happening and that it can give you joy.

We are naming familiar moments, which we all often encounter. But in order to feel that this is an event, it must be noticed, lived, and only then named.

Perhaps, after reading this book, you will become more aware of your feelings and will be able to find or remember words that are close to you and me.

I would like to come up with a word for the feeling of flight, or that tired feeling after skating when you take off your skates and your legs are suddenly very light!

And you? What feeling would you name?

Thanks to all the native speakers who have helped me find these words and check their translations, the photographers who inspired me to create the images of the countries I have never been to, and the close friends who supported me in everything.

I tried very hard to be accurate with all the definitions and translations, and I hope that if I made some mistakes, experts will forgive me.

Maria Ivashkina is an author, designer, and illustrator from Moscow, Russia. She opened her own children's publishing house in 2020, and this is the first book she has published. It was selected as a finalist for the prestigious Golden Pinwheel Award at the China Shanghai International Children's Book Fair.